Albert Fernandes

The importance of knowledge in the life of a Priest

GRIN Verlag

GRIN - Your knowledge has value

Since its foundation in 1998, GRIN has specialized in publishing academic texts by students, college teachers and other academics as e-book and printed book. The website www.grin.com is an ideal platform for presenting term papers, final papers, scientific essays, dissertations and specialist books.

Visit us on the internet:

http://www.grin.com/

http://www.facebook.com/grincom

http://www.twitter.com/grin_com

THE IMPORTANCE OF KNOWLEDGE IN THE LIFE OF THE PRIEST

Albert Fernandes

Seminar Paper

2010

Department of Indian Institute of Spirituality
St. Peter's Pontifical Institue, Bangalore, India

Contents

1. INTRODUCTION 3
2. WHAT IS KNOWLEDGE? 4
3. TYPES OF KNOWLEDGE 4
   - 3.1 SCIENCE AS KNOWLEDGE 4
   - 3.2 SELF KNOWLEDGE 5
   - 3.3 INTUITIVE KNOWLEDGE 5
   - 3.4 INFUSED KNOWLEDGE 5
4. UNDERSTANDING OF KNOWLEDGE IN CHRISTIANITY 6
   - 4.1 KNOWLEDGE IN THE BIBLE 6
   - 4.2 KNOWLEDGE IN CHRIST'S HUMAN INTELLECT 7
   - 4.3 KNOWLEDGE: THE GIFT OF THE HOLY SPIRIT 8
   - 4.4 CHURCH AND THE IMPORTANCE OF KNOWLEDGE 9
5. IMPORTANCE OF KNOWLEDGE IN THE LIFE OF A PRIEST 9
   - 5.1 KNOWLEDGE - THE EIGHTH SACRAMENT 9
   - 5.2 KNOWLEDGE OF THE CHURCH*S TEACHING AND DOCTRINE, ... 10
   - 5.3 STUDY AND PASTORAL KNOWLEDGE 10
   - 5.4 AS A PROPHET - DECLARES THE MESSAGE OF GOD 11
   - 5.5 AS A SHEPHERD - GUARDS THE FLOCK 11
   - 5.6 AS A TEACHER AND PREACHER - COMMUNICATES THE WORD OF GOD 12
   - 5.7 CONSTANT UPDATE - READING THE SIGNS OF THE TIMES 12
   - 5.8 KNOWLEDGE OF LOVE - 'HEART TO HEART' 13
6. CONCLUSION 14

1. Introduction

Now-a-days many priests and religious spend a major part of their early lives in studies of various kinds. They attend renewal programmes and crash courses during the vacations. They go through secular professional courses to ensure that they are equipped to be at the best service of humanity, especially those; the poor, the down trodden, those victimized and marginalized by the society and those who face injustice. For any further information they use the internet which is the easiest source of finding knowledge; which provides an almost unlimited magnitude of knowledge which was not available a few years ago. There has been a drastic change in the societal education system die to intense development in the multimedia and technologies. The knowledge that we have at a moment needs upgrading, since the latest version of the technology has upgraded the previous versions. One needs to be fast and even super fast to cope with the world that is going ahead with research in science and technology. Research and knowledge will make only little sense if it is not practical. Knowledge in the Christian perspective is the knowledge of God who revealed the eternal knowledge to humankind. We are called to mobilize our knowledge in the light of the knowledge of Christ Jesus who is the Revelation of God's knowledge to us. The priest who is the vicar of Christ, has to be filled with the knowledge of God and the medium of communicating the word to his people in an intelligent and reasonable way.

Today, knowledge of all kinds is possible and easily accessible. Social media and Internet makes things happen online and offline. We need to have knowledge about all this. Every priest must ask himself whether he is knowledgeable. How-a-days the members of the community are more knowledgeable than their priests and leaders when it comes to the academic achievements. Earlier centuries and years priests were the ones who brought knowledge to them and the educational institutions. Today there is a lot of competition from university to university to offers various types of courses and upgrading the lessons and topics of teaching according to the needs of the times. Many a times it is difficult for the priest who does not have the updated knowledge of the times to discuss the matters of concern with the people of the community. If the leader of the community is not knowledgeable enough then the members would not find him relevant to listen and attend to their problems.

Since the people are literate and well educated, the priest has to communicate the word of God in an intelligent and knowledgeable way. The exegeses of the word of God should touch the heart and mind of the people in such a way that they can understand in and through their life experiences, strives, and struggles. Therefore, to communicate the word of God in an effective manner from their cultural and traditional perspective, the priest must be knowledgeable in every aspect of the faith and belief and sacraments and be able to discern the will of God for the people. His teachings of the scriptures, church documents, and faith should be relevant in the times.

Therefore, the priest must be a leader of knowledge. In this paper, I wish to present the importance of knowledge in the life of a priest today. I will be dealing with the understanding of knowledge in Hinduism, Islam and Christianity in particular. Looking at the importance given to knowledge in the Old Testament, New Testament and in the life of Jesus; how important is knowledge for a priest today who is a priest, king and a prophet to the world for the sake of Christ.

2. What is Knowledge?

Knowledge by its very nature is beyond the horizon of knowing.[1] No knowledge can give you a comprehensive understanding of reality. Knowledge implicitly indicates what is not yet known. 'The most obvious form of knowledge involves human persons through the sense organs of sight, hearing, taste, smell, and touch as they encounter objects outside themselves."[2] Since knowledge is common to both animals and humankind, it is different from intellectual knowledge. Through science and philosophy which use reason and experience to understand the surrounding reality, human knowledge is constantly on the increase. Can everything be known? Knowledge acquisition involves complex cognitive processes: perception, learning, communication, association and reasoning.

The term *knowledge* is also used to mean the confident understanding of a subject with the ability to use it for a specific purpose. Knowledge can be basically categorized into the following types: knowledge of the senses, intellectual knowledge, spiritual knowledge, infused knowledge, acquired knowledge, self-knowledge, supernatural knowledge, interpretative knowledge, religious knowledge, intuitive knowledge and so on. There is no one theory of knowledge but immense variety of rival theories. 'Theory of knowledge is a misnomer, it is not a theory only about the nature of knowing and the objects of knowledge, if it has any pretentions to completeness, it must be a theory about the range and limits of knowing, and about what happens beyond those limits."[3] Knowledge is not limited to few selected sources but is widened to reach new and less known ones. "We live in a world of repressed and homogenized systems of knowledge which suppresses alternative sources of knowledge outside the established orthodoxy. We just cannot be content with knowledge associated with the theoretical process of objectivation, institutionalization and legitimization."[4]

3. Types of Knowledge

3.1 Science as Knowledge

Search for truth is the fundamental task of science. The researcher who moves on this plane of science feels all the more fascinated to know the truth. "Pure science is good in itself which deserves to be greatly loved, for it is knowledge, the perfection of human beings in their intelligence. Even before its technical applications, it should be loved for itself, as an integral part of human culture."[5] In scientific research, Galileo perceived the presence of the Creator who stimulates it, anticipates and assists its intuitions by acting in the very depths of its spirit.[6] Second Vatican Council teaches, "Methodological research, in all domains of

---

[1] Knowledge is an act of understanding: information fined through learning or actual experience. An intellectual virtue. A gift of the Holy Spirit. Cfr. Albert J. Nevins (ed.): *The Maryknoll Catholic Dictionary.* New York: Dimension Books.
[2] Michael Downey (ed.): *The New Dictionary of Catholic Spirituality.* Bangalore: Theological Publications in India, 1995, pp. 586.
[3] A. D. Woozley: *Theory of Knowledge.* London: Hutchinson University Library. 1966, pp. 10-11.
[4] Felix Wilfred, "Knowledge Ethics for Our Times." In: *Jeevadhara,* XXXIX, No.229
[5] Dennis J. Murphy (ed.): *The Church and the Bible: Official Documents of the Catholic Church.* Bangalore: Theological Publications in India, 2007, (no. 1050), p. 432.
[6] Ibid., (no. 1059), p. 436.

knowledge, if it follows moral norms, will never really be opposed to faith; both the realities of this world and of the faith find their origin in the same God".[7]

3.2 Self Knowledge

Knowledge of oneself is very important. St. Francis de Sales in the *Conference* states: "the first degree of humility is the knowledge of ourselves. It is consciousness that we have, when by personal experience and through the light of God's grace illumining our spirit we come to know that we are poor, wretched and worthless."[8] The light of divine grace is very important to know and see ourselves. Of course there should be genuine self-knowledge. Self knowledge is a lifelong process, once one has begun the journey and insights begin to flow, there comes simultaneously knowledge of who God is. For Karl Rahner, God's revelation of divine being is spoken of as God's self communication to the world through Christ in the power of the Holy Spirit.[9]

Francis de Sales affirms that 'know yourself not only means to know our unworthiness, imperfections and wretchedness, but also to become aware of the value and positive dimension of ourselves. This leads a person to trust in God's goodness and mercy. The knowledge of our nothingness should not trouble us but it should make us gentle, humble and lowly. Self knowledge implies a clear view of our meanness and weaknesses as well as the blessings and goodness we possess. Knowing our miseries and shortcomings should nurture us in humility. This self-knowledge should not make us sad nor discourage us but on the contrary it helps us to see these shortcomings as the throne of divine mercy.[10]

3.3 Intuitive Knowledge

It is a kind of epistemological pattern that is found in religious knowledge. The believer discovers divine events in history, that is, one *interprets* historical events in a certain way and reads in them the action of God. It is to say that "the revelatory events leave room for the spontaneous response called faith and preserve the cognitive freedom of the believers. Religious faith has the particular quality of being both cognitive and free because it is the voluntary recognition of God's activity in human history."[11] The intellect and the will have a part to play in the religious interpretation of events. To weigh up the above view that regards religious knowledge as interpretative knowledge, we should say that such characterization is correct but also inconsequential because every kind of knowledge involves an element of interpretation. Of course it does not rule out the possibility of being different from other types of knowledge.

3.4 Infused Knowledge

The Knowledge which is not dependent on personal effort in its acquisition but which is received as a gift is designated as infused knowledge. "It differs from acquired knowledge gained through the senses of the intellect insofar as God takes hold of the soul and teaches it. However the infused knowledge also differs from connatural knowledge because knowledge

---

[7] Ibid., (no. 1058), cfr. *Second Vatican* Council Document, *Goudium et Spes* § 36).
[8] Cfr. John Sankarathll: *Humility and Gentleness: Theological Investigations in the Writings of SL Francis de Sales.* Bangalore: Asian Trading Corporation, 2009, pp. 111; also cfr. *Conferences* of St. Francis de Sales.
[9] Karl Rahner: *Foundations of the Christian Faith.* W. Dych (trans.). New York: Scribner's. 1959, pp. 116-119.
[10] John Sankarathil, pp. 113-114.
[11] Ibid., p. 29

by con-naturality assumes an association with the intellect."[12] Therefore it is understandable that infused knowledge can be explained as the means by which God offers self disclosure to humankind.

4 Understanding of Knowledge in Christianity

4.1 Knowledge in the Bible

The key biblical terms for knowledge assume a personal familiarity, especially knowing with clarity and completeness, even an intimate involvement, with the known object. Similarly, knowing God entails acknowledging Him as Lord in obedience and praise. As a result, human knowledge of God is decisively shaped by the fall and God's salvation.

The Bible teaches that truth has its ontological ground in God Himself (Ps 31:5; Isa 65:16; Jn 146).[13] All human knowledge is dependent upon God, who is the source and stipulator of truth. During the earthly ministry, Jesus was encouraged and sustained by His unique knowledge of the Father (Jn 8:55).[14]

Adam and Eve knew God. They acknowledged him as their Lord and obediently carried out their responsibilities as his stewards in creation. However, eating from the forbidden tree of the knowledge of good and evil decisively shaped humanity's future (Gen 2:9 Gen 2:17). The knowledge derived from eating this fruit is called godlike (Gen 3:5 Gen 3:22), denoting a rebellious attempt to decide good and evil independently of the Creator.

The fall, however, did not destroy the availability of God's knowledge. General revelation, God's universal revelation, still exists. After the fall, saving knowledge of God is grounded solely in God's , decision to reveal himself to sinners (Gen 18:18-19; Ex 33:17; Ps 139; Jer 1:5; Eph3:35). In these Acts of special revelation, God chooses a people for his purposes and guides them back to himself (Amos 3:2).For sinners can come into fellowship with God only through God's prior act, which objectively makes known his mercy, and subjectively makes us rightly related to Him.

Human knowledge is likewise a theme of the Old Testament. Mankind is enjoined not to glory in wisdom, might, or riches, -but in the privilege of knowing God (Jer 9:23f). God was the Supreme reality to believers of the Old Testament era, even though at times they experienced difficulty in understanding the dispensations of His providence (Job 19:25f).[15]

Knowledge of God frequently depends on the witness of others to whom God has revealed himself (Ps 44:1-4; Is 51:1- 2). Only those who know God may seek him. In the New Testament* for example, the first step toward knowledge consists of receiving Jesus' message (Jn 7:16-17; 12:37-46; 20:30-31). Only those-willing to believe that Jesus is doing the will of the Father receive the light enabling them to discern that he is the Son of God. On

---

[12] Michael Downey, p. 586.
[13] To keep up to the consistency of the scriptural passages and language all throughout the paper. I have used for scriptural references New Revised Standard Version, Catholic Edition, Bangalore: Theological Publications In India, 2009.
[14] Geoffrey W. Bromiley: *The International Standard Bible Encyclopedia.* Vol III, K-P. Michigan: William B. Eedmans Publishing Company, 1992, p.,49.
[15] Geoffrey W. Bromiley, p. 48.

this path, followers are led to the full truth. Sinners, on the other hand, come to a knowledge of God through judgment and repentance. In repentance one recognizes the holy God who demands righteousness (Ps 25:14; 111:10; Prov 1:7; 2:5; 9:10).

If knowledge of God is the path of our life, this must manifest itself in godly relationships to others (Mt 7:17-20; Jn 10:27; 1 Cor 12:31-13:2; Phil 4:9; Col 1:23). "We know that we have come to know him if we obey his commands" (1 Jn 2:3). Those who know God willingly practice his will and thus manifest his character by defending the cause of the poor (Jer 22:16 ; Hos 6:6). In addition, the one following God's path becomes a co-worker for God's kingdom (Is 43:10-12).

Reflecting the messianic promise of knowledge (Jer 24:7; 31:33-34), there is a finality to the Christian's knowledge of God (Mt 11:27; Rom 16:25-27; Eph 1:9-10; Coll:26-28). In Christ "are hidden all the treasures of wisdom and knowledge" (Col 2:3). Moreover, in contrast to ordinary historical knowledge, this knowledge of God is self-authenticating. God himself personally confronts each Individual in the Word (2 Cor 4:6; 1 Jn 2:27), foreshadowing the future when teaching is no longer necessary (Jer 31:34 }. "All human knowledge is dependent upon God, who is the source and stipulator of truth."[16]

On the other hand, the believer's knowledge of God in Jesus Christ is only provisional. It is sufficient for recognizing and trusting the object of faith (Jn 17:3; Rom 10:9): "I know my sheep and my sheep know me... My sheep listen to my voice" (Jn 10:14, 27).Without answering all our questions, it provides an adequate light for the journeyers in this darkened world (2 Pet 1:19). But this knowledge is only a foretaste of knowing God "face to face" in the hereafter (1 Cor 13:12), when "the day dawns and the morning star arises in your hearts" (2 Pet 1:19).[17]

4.2 Knowledge in Christ's Human Intellect

Knowledge of Jesus Christ here does not mean a summary of what we know about Jesus Christ, but a survey of the intellectual endowment of Christ.

Jesus Christ possessed two natures, and therefore two intellects, the human and the Divine. The question as to the knowledge found in His Divine intellect is identical with the question concerning God's knowledge.

The Man-God possessed, not merely a Divine, but also a human nature, and therefore a human intellect, and with the knowledge possessed by this intellect we are here mainly concerned. The integrity of His human nature implies intellectual cognition by acts of its human intellect. Jesus Christ might be wise by the wisdom of God; yet the humanity of Christ knows by its own mental act. For the soul of Christ enjoyed from the very beginning the beatific vision; it was endowed with infused knowledge; and it acquired in the course of time experimental knowledge.

The existence of an infused science in the human soul of Jesus Christ may perhaps be less certain, from a theological point of view, than His continual and original fruition of the vision

---

[16] Ibid., p. 49.
[17] Walter A. Elwell (ed.). *Knowledge of God.* In: "Evangelical Dictionary of Theology". Michigan: Baker Books, 1997. - Standing: 11.11.2009. - http: // www.biblestudytools.com /dictionaries/bakers-evangelical-dictionarv/knowl- edge-of-god.html - Electronic Publications.

of God; still, it is almost universally admitted that God infused into Christ's human intellect a knowledge similar in kind to that of the angels. This is knowledge which is not acquired gradually by experience, but is poured into the soul in one flood.

Besides, the soul of Christ is the first and most perfect of all created spirits, and cannot be deprived of a privilege granted to the angels. Moreover, a created intellect is simply perfect only when, besides the vision of things in God, it has a vision of things in themselves; God only sees all things comprehensively in Himself. The God-Man, besides seeing them in God, would also perceive and know them by His human intellect. Finally, Sacred Scripture favours the existence of such infused knowledge in the human intellect of Christ: St. Paul speaks of all the treasures of God's wisdom and science hidden in Christ (Col 2:3); Isaiah speaks of the spirit of wisdom and counsel, of science and understanding, resting on Jesus (Is 11:2); St. John intimates that God has not given His Spirit by measure to His Divine envoy (Jn 3:34); St. Matthew represents Christ as our sovereign teacher (Mt 23:10).

4.3 Knowledge: The Gift of the Holy Spirit

In many expressions of Christianity, knowledge is one of the seven gifts of the Holy Spirit. The update of the knowledge is very important. Pope John Paul II, encourages the theologians to go ahead with theological research and exhorts them to take notice of the queries and needs of the *times* without letting oneself go astray by fortuitous and short-lived currents of the human mind. Scientific and in particular theological knowledge needs courage to venture and the patience of maturity. It has its own laws and must not be allowed to be imposed from without.[18]

"We are called upon to encounter science, and with it the whole earth, nature and the cosmos in our search through heaven and earth for the Lord of all. God's spirit wants to imbue all faculties of man with his living grace, and so it consecrates science too placing it among the gifts."[19] The aim of science is to teach us how to think rightly about all created things, but beyond objects we move on to the relationships between them. "Science is the study of relationship, cause and effect, premises and consequences, data and theorems, etc., but the mind goes on ordering, conquering categories, acquiring names." However knowledge is much more than science because everything of science cannot be comprehended since science is more of signs and equations but it also gives the knowledge about the purpose of God's creation.

Knowledge allows us to see the circumstances of our life as God sees them, although in a more limited way, since we are limited by our human nature. Through the exercise of knowledge, we can ascertain God's purpose in our lives and His reason for placing us in our particular circumstances. Knowledge is sometimes called the science of the saints, because it enables those who have the gift to discern easily and effectively between the impulses of temptation and the inspirations of grace. Judging all things in. the light of divine truth, we can more easily distinguish between the promptings of God and the subtle wiles of the devil.[20]

---

[18] Dennis J. Murphy (edj; *The Church and the Bible: Official Documents of the Catholic Church,* no. 1063, pp. 437-438.

[19] Carlos G. Valles: *Taste and See: Gifts and Fruits of the Holy Spirit.* Anand: - Gujrat Sahitya Prakash, 1990, p. 61.

[20] Ibid., pp. 62-65.

4.4 Church and the Importance of Knowledge

Knowledge is the norm of rule in every human being in the society and religion. Knowledge is not something to acquire speculatively, but to attain with methodological research and understanding. The church always gave importance to those who made research in bettering the faith of every Christian faithful. The learned and the wise could do any research taking into consideration its moral concerns. The word of God is passed on from one generation to another with intelligence and knowledge. If the word of God was not preserved and wound up with the signs of the times, then the humans, out of ignorance, would have forgotten and would make the word of God irrelevant for the present times.

The church shows special concern to those who . impart this knowledge in preaching the word of God in an exegetical form. Church believes that "those who have transmitted the Gospel to us have preached the Gospel. Haying followed the will of God, they transmitted it to us in the Scriptures so that it would be the pillar and mainstay of our faith; In reality, after our Lord had risen from the dead and they had received the power of the Spirit from above, they were filled with all gifts and had perfect knowledge."[21]

5. Importance of Knowledge in the Life of a Priest

A priest is a Vicar of Christ. He is the representative of the community entrusted to him. He has a lot of responsibilities upon him. He is a man of the community who can either build the community or destroy the community. The community looks at him with great reverence for knowledge and spiritual guidance. He is a man whom people consider the representative of God. Therefore a priest must know his responsibilities well. He is a man of knowledge; of the scriptures, of the Kingdom of God, the morals of the society, and the knowledge of science. It is a knowledge where in the knower becomes like unto the known.

In other terms he is a 'Presbyter' or 'elder' denotes the function of a spiritual leader of the community of the People of God and hence the term denotes the functions of sanctifying, teaching and ruling.[22]

5.1 Knowledge - The Eighth Sacrament

For a priest knowledge is so necessary that it is almost like the eighth sacrament as St. Francis de sales mentions in his writings.[23] Therefore he insists that those who hold authority in the Church, especially, the Pope, the Bishops and the priests should be well educated and

---

[21] Dennis J. Murphy (ed.): *The Church and the Bible: Official Documents of the Catholic Church.* no. 756, p. 323; see also Instruction, *Sancta Mater Ecclesia,* concerning the historical truth of the Gospels: AAS 56 *(1964)* 712-718. Translated by Joseph A. Fitzmyer in *Theological Studies,*25(1964), pp. 386-408.

[22] Thomas Pazhayampallil: *Pastoral* Guide: Sacraments and *Ethics.* Vol. 2, Bangalore: Kristu Jyoti Publications, 1995, pp. 444-445.

[23] It is very much true as St. Francis de Sales says that , the failures in the consecrated life of the clergy and the religious and the consequent de-formation of character and conviction, is largely due to the lack of knowledge of the consecrated persons themselves regarding the committed life, which they have undertaken, and the consequent loss of the sense of priority in life. As quoted •by Benni Gregoriose Koottanal: Eucharist is *Love: A Dogmatic and Hermeneutic Understanding of the Salesian Eucharistic Theology in the Calvinistic Bra.* London: Transaction Publishers, 2005, pp. 258-259; Francois de Sales: *[Euvres de Saint Francois de Sales: Eveque et Prince de Geneve et Docteur de L'Eglise.* Vol. XXIII, / publiee par les soins des Religieuses se autographes et les editions originals. Annecy: Imprimere J. Nierat et al., 1892-1932, pp.303-305.

well equipped in the matters of faith, the church, and sacraments and even in civil matters that they will be able to communicate the truth, which they believe, effectively and convincingly. At the same time they should be able to resist the wrong teachings, which sprout up against the teachings of the Church.[24] The priest must not be ignorant of the events whether pleasant or unpleasant that takes place in the world. His interpretation of the scriptures for the faithful should consist in motivating them through his touch and sensitivity of the daily events that affect their lives.

5.2 Knowledge of the Church's Teaching and Doctrine,

A Sacred minister's knowledge ought to be sacred in the sense of being derived from a sacred source and directed to a sacred purpose. It is drawn from the reading and meditation of sacred scriptures. It is also nourished by the study of the Fathers and Doctors of the Church and the other ancient records of Tradition. They should be able to give adequate answers to the questions posed by the people at the present time. They should be well versed in the statements of the Church's magisterium and especially those of the Councils and the Popes.[25]

Being a teacher and preacher of faith, a priest needs to know all the basic teachings and doctrines of the Church. The updates of the faith and its new insights are to be brought to their knowledge with apt explanations and relevant interpretations. The laity has a right to knowledge from their priest and therefore he must have full knowledge of the Church's beliefs, teachings and doctrines.

5.3 Study and Pastoral Knowledge

Priests are instructed at the time of ordination by the bishops that they are to be 'mature in knowledge' and that their teaching should be 'a spiritual medicine for the people of God.'[26] The decree on Training of Priests mentions about the philosophy and theology subjects that are to be taught to the students for a solid and consistent knowledge of man, the world and God, relying on that philosophical patrimony which is forever valid, with the consideration of the knowledge of sciences too.[27]

The Council further discussed that "the Bishops should ensure that there will never be any

---

[24] In the present context of the Church and the society it is very much a need that the priest must have knowledge in all the fields of life. The faithful need to be guided rightly in the spirit of the scriptures and the knowledge in the world of fast growing technology and science. In terms of morality, it has been a question in the minds of the young and growing youth who are caught up by the world's clutches of immoral acts, in which case they need guidance and direction for discernment. St. Francis de Sales precisely makes the faithful are not led in ignorance of knowledge of God, of church's teachings and to-resist the bad in the world. As quoted by Benni Gregoriose Koottanal; pp. 258; Francois de Sales, (Euvres *de Saint Francois de Sales: Eveque et Prince de Geneve et Docteurde L'Eglise,* Vol. V, / publiee par les soins des Religieuses se autographes et les editions originals. Annecy: Imprimere J. Nierat et al., 1892-1932, pp.333- 334.

[25] Cfr. Austin Flannery (Ed.): Vatican *Council II: The Counciliar and Post Counciliar Documents.* Bandra: St. Paul's Publications, 1995, pp.788-789; cfr. also *Roman pontifical:* "Ordination of a Priest." cfr. also conc. Vat II: *Dei Verbum,* "On Divine Revelation." no.25, 18 November 1965, cfr. also conc. Vat II, *Presbyterorum Ordinis,* no. 19, 7 December, 1956.

[26] Cfr. "Lumen Gentium: Dogmatic Constitution on the Church." no. 65. In: *Vatican Council It The Counciliar and Post Councilia* Documents / Austin Flannery (ed.). Bombay: St. Paul's Publications, 1995.

[27] Cfr. conc. Vat II: Presbyterorum *Ordinis,* no. 15.7 December, 1956, p. 789.

lack of suitable teachers for the education of clerics, which will also ensure that the rest of the priests and the faithful will be helped to acquire the knowledge of religion necessary. for them, and that the sound progress in sacred studies so very necessary for the Church will be encouraged."[28] The other theological subjects should be renewed through a more vivid contact with the Mystery of Christ and the history of the church. Special care should be given to' moral theology; its scientific presentation should draw more fully on the teaching of Holy Scripture and should throw light upon the exalted vocation of the faithful in Christ and their obligation to bring forth fruit in charity for the life of the world. In the same way the study of the canon law and church history should be given importance.[29]

5.4 As a Prophet - Declares the Message of God

Many a time we see the world and one another the way we choose to see them, not the way God sees them. And so it hints that we might also see God the way we are, not the way God is. The prophet interrupts, intervenes and jolts us into uncertainly of doubt and directly points out with courage. The prophet intends only on stopping us, if only momentarily so that God's word can censure us, threaten us, and call us to repentance and transformation.[30]

5.5 As a Shepherd - Guards the Flock

To guard means, it is understood, that one has the capacity to protect, to watch and be vigilant. The shepherd would always be vigilant to keep the enemy and the fox away from its flock. The flock finds security and trust the shepherd that under his protection there is no fear of the enemy. When we apply this theory to the Priest as a shepherd, what do we find in the present times? One needs to know the flock first so that as per the need they could be attended to. The shepherd studies every sheep and knows the need of each one. When the weak and the sick need his help he carries them on his shoulders so that they don't get drowned in the shadow of the darkness.

Jesus gives this mission to Peter with a great challenge. Till he gets the full knowledge of his responsibility, the Lord keeps questioning him. "*Simon son of John, do you love me more than these... Feed my lambs... Tend my Sheep.*" Third time again he asked him and he said, "Feed my Sheep" (Jn 21:15-17).

Priest is a shepherd called to give life to his flock, called to have total knowledge of his flock so that his community will find security under his protection. Attending to the needs of the sick, the weak and the helpless is a must. In every parish there are men and women who live in isolation and despair. They need our visitation. They need someone to listen to them and understand them.[31] At times we think it is the knowledge of the science that is going to help us in our shepherding. Though scientific knowledge is necessary, it is more important to have the knowledge of understanding and feeling for the people entrusted to his care.

---

[28] Ibid., p. 789.
[29] Cfr. Austin Flannery (Ed.), p. 636-637; see also Couc. Vat II: *Optatam Tatius,* Decree on the Training of Priests,' nos. 14-15, 28 October, 1965.
[30] Megan McKenna: Prophets: Words of Fire. Bandra: Pauline Sisters Society, 2002, pp. 15-17.
[31] Arthur L. Teikmanis: *Preaching and Pastoral Care.* Philadelphia: Fortress Press, 1968, pp. 24-25.

5.6 As a Teacher and Preacher - Communicates the Word of God

Teaching and preaching need dynamism in communication. The communicator should have the knowledge of ways and means to, communicate the message in an effective way. An effective preacher and teacher should have full knowledge about his subjects and moreover he should have "right attitudes with integrity and morality, open-mindedness, fairness, courage and maturity."?[32] As a teacher of the community the priest should have knowledge of the 'Kingdom of God," that he is going to preach to them. One cannot give to the other what one does not have; therefore one must make oneself worthy and knowledgeable of the Kingdom of God. Vima Dasan writes:

> It is surely true that many professing Christians do not want to hear sound doctrine. They want to hear only sermons that will not challenge their sinful desires. They do not want to hear about the wrongness of their worldliness. .They, do not want their lack of righteousness revealed. They do not want to be confronted with the need of being born again. Yet, St.Paul insists that precisely because our time is such, we must preach, being alert and watchful in all things, enduring all afflictions and continuing to do the work of an evangelist.[33]

However Knowledge is power, "the preacher must have deep knowledge of religious truth and if possible an expert knowledge of the particular subject on which he happens to preach. In. addition, good knowledge of human nature, of human life and human conditions would greatly help him to see a religious truth in its proper light."[34] We can give to the other only what we have. "The intimate relationship of a priest to Christ is the foundation of his relationship with the Church."[35]

A priest must be an effective, teacher and preacher making use of the various channels of communication that are at his disposal. The vocal, facial and experiential level expressions are to be used with the modem technology of conveying the message. There are also other technical channels that a priest must have knowledge of and must acquire the skill in it:

5.7 Constant Update - Reading the Signs of the Times

Seminary life is the time of promoting knowledge for the candidates to priesthood. "Both philosophical and theological training enables the candidate to make a right co-ordination and interpretation of faith and reflection. Thus the seminarians grow from the state of theology students to that of theologians."[36]

Knowledge cannot be acquired in totality. The more we know, the more we understand how less we know. Therefore the attitude of humility is very important before knowledge. It does not matter how much we know, but what matters is what we know.

The decree on the training of Priests explains: "the priestly training in view of the circumstances of modern society, should be continued and perfected after the completion of the seminary course, it will be the task of Episcopal conferences in each country to provide

---

[32] Vima Dasan: *Preaching Sharp*. Bangalore: ATC Publications, 2007, p. 11.
[33] Vima Dasan, pp. 10-11.
[34] Ibid., p. 34.
[35] Jacob Parappally: "To be a Christ to-the Community; Challenges to Priestly Life and Ministry." In: *Vaiharat* Vol. 14, No. 1, 2009, p. 17
[36] Joshy Mayyattil: "Priest of Tomorrow: An outline for Priestly Formation Based on the Spirituality of St. John Marie Viaimey." In: *The Living Word*, Vol. 115, No.4, (2009), pp. 229.

the appropriate means for its continuation... in their spiritual, intellectual and pastoral aspects, with opportunities for constant update and progress."[37][37] Various religious institutions conduct renewal programmes for the priests who are busy the whole year in their apostolate. Every priest must take a chance to receive this knowledge of update to be relevant for the need of the ministry of the times.

5.8 Knowledge of Love - 'Heart to Heart'

Knowledge of any expertise is seen in one's action and thus we call the person a professional.[38] However one does not become professional with theoretical knowledge but one becomes professional with applied knowledge, called 'knowledge in action.' But for a priest it is not his knowledge of the skill that will prove him to be effective in the ministry but the integration of knowledge and his way of life. "The intellect may seek God, but it is the heart that finds Him."[39] Love for reading and learning, and openness to new values, experiences and approaches should be promoted in the value based education of the priests.

Our knowledge should not Only widen the intellectual world perspective but more over it should affect the knowledge of the heart. One must learn to love the other in charily and faith. Knowledge, if it is not personalized and exercised in a charitable manner, will not affect the heart rather it will be only the activity of the mind. John Main writes:

> For Paul, Knowledge is not power, as though to know God is to have power over Him, or as though knowing God gives us power over others. The only .'power' he talks of is that of kingdom and vision, gifts not tools, which lead to authentic knowledge. Personal knowledge of something is objective. To know someone is not knowing something about them, which might give you power over them. Knowing is to be one with. Therefore knowledge is going beyond and being one with the other. Knowledge as love is to discover myself one with a reality greater than I am alone.[40]

However, every priest must strive to make use of his knowledge and experience of joy in his concern for the people entrusted to him.

---

[37] Austin Flannery (Ed.), p. 641; see also Coun. Vat II: *OptatamTotius,* Decree on the Training of Priests, no. 22, 28 October, 1965.

[38] Positively, both Scripture and the Greek philosophical tradition understood knowledge as a form of intimate participation in which the knower becomes like unto the known. A matter of the heart as well as the head, such knowledge is transformative and life-giving when that which is known is the living God. Often times negatively, knowledge is defined more narrowly and ascribed value only within strict limits. Augustine located knowledge within the realm of action and distinguished it from the wisdom proper to contemplation, because 'wisdom is concerned with the intellectual cognizance of eternal things and knowledge with the rational cognizance of temporal things'. Thomas Kempis asked whether knowledge was of any use at all apart from the fear of God. The Apostle Paul counted knowledge as a spiritual gift but did not think it among the highest gifts, warning that /knowledge puffs up, but love builds up. Cfr. Philip Sheldrake, *The New SCM Dictionary of Christian Spirituality,* London: SCM Press Ltd., 2005, p. 396.

[39] Joshy Mayyattil, p. 229.

[40] John Main: *The Way of Unknowing:* Bangalore: IIS Publications. 2003, pp. 70-71.

6. Conclusion

We have seen the types of knowledge and how they affect the life of the priest who is a leader, councillor, shepherd, guide and teacher of a community with persons of various calibre and knowledge. The world dominated by the multinational technologies and solutions give variety of choices to the young people with opportunities to learn and earn well. However one tends to think that knowing well means earning well. In the life of a priest it is just the opposite. He does not acquire knowledge for earning for himself but rather to lose oneself. The life of a priest is all about self-sacrificing. He learns and acquires knowledge not for himself but for the betterment of the community. He does not choose what he *must* learn but the situations teach him what he should learn.

Every priest must understand that his primary duty is to continue the works of Christ. Christ gave Himself totally to God with full knowledge of God and His people. He had the knowledge of the society, religion, traditions and culture of the times. He appreciated the good traditions but brought renewal to those which were irrelevant and only ritualistic. He was a person who understood the will of God with total knowledge of God. He had knowledge of the people around Him and with whom he lived and proclaimed 'the Good News of the Kingdom of God.' He knew the mission that He had to accomplish. He kept up to the relevance of his knowledge with total confidence in the Father. He relied on the true knowledge that is God the Father. Therefore His experience of God as Abba tells us how close He was and how closely He related to the Father in full knowledge of Him.

Every priest is called to possess knowledge of faith and science which can be used to relate to God and to humanity. Being a leader, shepherd, teacher and preacher, he needs to have up-to-date knowledge of the scripture, church's teachings and doctrines, and of humanity, world and science. Integration of all these aspects of knowledge in life situations for a healthy faith is called knowledge. Without the knowledge of faith and belief our hearts will not speak of the wonders of the Lord. Our knowledge should help the faithful to grow in their daily aspirations in following Christ Jesus. Priest is a man who sets apart some time for reading and assimilating the knowledge that he gets through the media of the times and executes it in an intelligent way to his receivers.

Sunday homilies and daily instructs based on the scripture need to be scholarly in terms of knowledge and lived in daily life. The priest should have the capacity of integrating the knowledge that he has for the well being of the people entrusted to him. He should impart to them knowledge that will produce and bear good fruits that will abide.